ALSO BY BILLY COLLINS

POETRY

Sailing Alone Around the Room
Nine Horses
The Trouble with Poetry
Ballistics
Horoscopes for the Dead
Aimless Love
The Rain in Portugal
Whale Day
Musical Tables

ANTHOLOGIES

Poetry 180: A Turning Back to Poetry
180 More: Extraordinary Poems for Every Day
Bright Wings: An Anthology of Poems About Birds

Water, Water

Water, Water

BILLY COLLINS

RANDOM HOUSE

NEW YORK

Published in the United States by Random House, an imprint
and division of Penguin Random House LLC, New York.

RANDOM HOUSE and the HOUSE colophon are registered
trademarks of Penguin Random House LLC.

LIBRARY OF CONGRESS CATALOGING-IN-PUBLICATION DATA
Names: Collins, Billy, author.
Title: Water, water : poems / by Billy Collins.
Description: First edition. | New York : Random House, 2024.
Identifiers: LCCN 2024005981 (print) |
LCCN 2024005982 (ebook) | ISBN 9780593731024 (hardcover) |
ISBN 9780593731031 (ebook)
Subjects: LCGFT: Poetry.
Classification: LCC PS3553.O47478 W38 2024 (print) |
LCC PS3553.O47478 (ebook) |
DDC 811/.54—dc23/eng/20240214
LC record available at https://lccn.loc.gov/2024005981
LC ebook record available at https://lccn.loc.gov/2024005982

Printed in the United States of America on acid-free paper

randomhousebooks.com

2 4 6 8 9 7 5 3 1

First Edition

Book design by Caroline Cunningham
Title page and part opener water ornament: iStock/drawlab19

For
John Stravinsky
who lived the sporting life
(1945–2023)

Water, water, every where,

And all the boards did shrink;

Water, water, every where,

Nor any drop to drink.

—COLERIDGE, "The Rime of the
Ancient Mariner"

Contents

Two

Three

Four

Winter Trivia

*It takes approximately two hours for a snowflake to fall
from a cloud to the ground.*
—THE BOOK OF TRIVIA

In the roughly two hours
it takes for a snowflake
to fall from a cloud to the ground,

we managed to get back to the house,
bang the snow off our boots,
shake out our coats in the mudroom,

then stoke the stove back to life,
open a bottle of wine—
I think it was a red from Oregon—

heat the white bean soup from last night,
which we spooned up
sitting close to the splintering stove,

after which we carried our bowls
to the kitchen and opened
an inlaid wooden box full of chips

and fanned out a fresh deck of playing cards,
which you shuffled and I cut,
as the house was warming up,

and you tossed in a modest bet
with a red Jack showing
and I saw you with my nine

just as that singular snowflake
landed without a sound
in the general darkness of Vermont.

One

Fire

I'm having a swell time reading *Lonesome Dove,*
glad I still have 400 pages to go,
but this paperback is one
of a thousand things around me
I would not grab as I dashed into the street
if the house ever decided to burst into flames.

I probably couldn't find the cat
for all the smoke filling every room,
so let me see, give me a minute . . .

I should have thought of this earlier
before the fire trucks arrived
and men in helmets were rushing past me.

But here I am out on the lawn in a bathrobe
with a few sleepy neighbors,
red lights flashing all over us.
I'm holding a photograph to my chest
and the cat is sitting next to me,
apparently mesmerized by the flames.

I'm happy with my choice
as I look down at you and me in a frame.
Here's a chance for a fresh start, I figure.
And as for the ashes of *Lonesome Dove,*
I can always get another copy, or maybe
that's just where I was meant to stop reading.

Marijuana

When I was young and dreamy,
I longed to be a poet,
not one with his arms
wrapped around the universe
or on his knees before a goddess,
not waving from Mount Parnassus
nor wearing a cape like Lord Byron,
rather just reporting on a dog or an orange.

But one soft night in California
I walked outside during a party,
lay down on the lawn
beneath a lively sky,
and after an interlude of nonstop gazing,
I happened to swallow the moon,
yes, I opened my mouth in awe
and swallowed the full moon whole.

And the moon dwelled within me
when I returned to the lights of the party,
where I was welcomed back

with understanding and hilarity
and was recognized long into the night
as *The Man Who Swallowed the Moon,*
he who had walked out of a storybook
and was dancing now with a girl in the kitchen.

Ode to Joy

Friedrich Schiller called Joy *the spark of divinity,*
but she visits me on a regular basis,
and it doesn't take much for her to appear—
the salt next to the pepper by the stove,
the garbage man ascending his station
on the back of the moving garbage truck,
or I'm just eating a banana
in the car and listening to Buddy Guy.

In other words, she seems down to earth,
like a girl getting off a bus with a suitcase
and no one's there to meet her.
It's a little after 4 in the afternoon,
one of the first warm days of spring.
She sits on her suitcase to wait
and slides on her sunglasses.
How do I know she's listening to the birds?

While in Amsterdam

With a good ten days to burn,
I figured it would be a mortal sin
if I failed to pay a visit
to the site of Chet Baker's death,
perhaps even end up in jazz hell
if I did not stand for a while
beneath the hotel window
out of which he was pushed
by a jealous woman, or simply fell.

You might ask about "jazz hell."
I never gave it any thought
until I made it up just now.
I don't like the sound of the jazz violin.
It always sounded like a violinist
had wandered into the wrong
recording studio and just
started playing along with the others,
only slower and not as well.

So my personal jazz hell
would have to be an all–violin band,
each solo lasting eternally,
so only one violin would
ever improvise while the infinite
number of other violins
would comp in the background
and play as improperly loud
as the constant ringing of bells.

All of which leaves me glad
that we finally did walk there
in a light rain and did stand
on that unfeeling pavement
below that fatal window.
We even had our photograph taken
next to the plaque of Chet Baker,
blowing his trumpet in bas–relief,
eyes shut tight, just so we would have a story to tell.

ABCDEFGHIJKLMNOPQRSTUVWXYZ

It didn't take a lot of staring
at the alphabet embroidered
in a frame on the wall
of a doctor's waiting room
in letters round and straight, blue and orange,

before that cryptogram
began to look like a word in itself,
one long crush of sound and sense,
impossible to pronounce or comprehend.
Was this then the very first word

uttered by some god of language
in a yawp that later would be combined
into all the words we know,
the shorter ones we see every day
whether in a magazine or a poem by Amy Lowell?

But there's the nurse at the door
calling *William,* making me officially next,
and somehow reminding me

that the letters are there in order
for children lined up in school

to sing the notes of every letter
in a chorus of vowels and consonants,
or for you to say backwards
as you stand in the rain by your ticking car,
halted by the law in your rush to get from A to B.

Adam Names the Fish

Genesis 2:20

Exhausted,
after coming up with *giraffe,*
buffalo, and *butterfly,*
then *ocelot* and *kangaroo*
he begs the sky for a breather.

But there is nothing
but the silence
of the low clouds,
then a trace of wind,
the tweet of a *wren,*
the moo of a *cow,*

two of the many
he is most proud of
for their simplicity,
and the hint of onomatopoeia.
Cow. Wren.
He likes *snake* and *canary* too.

But the silence says
he has more work to do.
So, with nary an Eve to impress,
he takes the deepest breath
known to man,
and, holding it, dives in.

Magical Realism

It's a rainy Saturday night in London
and many of the male dogs
have gathered at their favorite pub,
the Ball and Stick,
where they lower their heads
to drink from their bowls of ale,
for this is not an off-the-wall cartoon,
where they would be leaning on the bar
holding a pint glass impossibly in one paw.

No, this is just a bit of fiction,
but not by a fantasist of South America,
where many strange things are done.
And that's why the dogs are not
smoking cigars or playing darts,
or gossiping about their owners.
Nor is there any laughter, no sports on the telly,
no back-slapping, which would require
standing up all night on your hind legs.

And that's also why it's so quiet
for a Saturday night with your mates,
unlike the clamor down the lane
at the Ax and Hammer,
or around the corner at the King's Piston.
Here, it's just the low sounds of lapping
and a round of barking every time
a new dog happens to walk in the door,
yes, on all fours and without a stitch of clothes.

Cough Drop

I'm in the paddock with my friend Niall
at Tampa Bay Downs.

The horses are getting saddled
while the jockeys pace in their silks,
and we're listening to Brenda, the trainer,
as she explains one way a horse can get into trouble.

How, alone in its stall, a racehorse
will sometimes roll onto its back
to stretch or scratch an itch
then flip all the way over and get its legs
stuck under one of the wooden slats.

Trapped by its own weight
and too heavy to be pulled back up,
the horse can panic and injure itself,
so what you do first is quiet it down,

Brenda told us in her Boston accent,
then slip on a bridle,

and ease the horse by the head
away from the wall and back up on its feet.

Now the jockeys were up
and guiding their mounts onto the soft track,
and I was thinking how fortunate
to have people in the world like Brenda,
who know exactly what to do and do it—
nurses and firemen, eye surgeons and harbor pilots.

Soon, the three of us were at the rail
as the field charged past in a colorful blur,
and the earth released a little tremble,
the crowd crescendoed, and the race was over.

Niall's horse faded and finished 4th,
and a filly I backed because of her name,
Cough Drop, came in second to last,

but luck was with the horses in that race
if only because all eight of them
were safe and whole at the finish—
not one down, trapped, or broken—
no need for Brenda or anyone
like her to come running with help.

Aubade

I'm in bed with one eye open
on a gloomy morning,
the room as shadowy as the one
in Larkin's wake-up poem,
and the light between the drapes
as grey as Whistler's sideways mother.

But once I slip into my Hawaiian slippers,
I sense an uptick about to occur,
perhaps caused by 3 oranges in a bowl,
or a man out for a run
with his pug hurrying behind
as I pull open the blinds in the front room.

It could be the lemon tree
bowing under the weight of lemons
that I see when swimming on my back,

or the big photo of Harriet Tubman
on a billboard everyone sped by,
or that skeleton of a rabbit

you pointed to one afternoon
in the dune grass with the surf crashing away.

Eventually, this thing or that
will get the day rolling
on the parallel rails of another month.

Then off we go, Mr. Wednesday and I,
waving as we slip around these many curves,

him a central feature of every future week,
me with one less day to live—
like Philip Larkin sitting up in bed,
alone and startled, his wall calendar in flames.

When a Man Loves Something

Late one night at a roadhouse
a little down from where I lived
on the edge of a California desert,
I happened to hear Percy Sledge live.

I remember his voice rising
to such heights of conviction that night,
I felt lucky to have spotted
his name on the lit-up yellow sign outside.

As I listened over my drink,
I silently wished him well
and extended that wish to Mrs. Sledge
and all the little Sledges
if there happened to be any around.

Years later, when I lived in Florida,
we had a plumber
whose name was Lynn Hammer.

I like to introduce people to one another,
but Lynn Hammer said
he had never heard of Percy Sledge
and put his head back under the sink.

So many miscues like that these days,
as when I remarked
in a store that featured fancy pastries,
"This isn't your grandmother's coffee shop!"

and the girl glanced up at me
as if I were from another planet,
which, of course, I was,
if the Past can be added
to the ones already orbiting the sun

including our small blue one,
which is carrying you and me
and everyone else,
along with the singer and the plumber,
the barista and yes, maybe even her grandmother,
in a big oval somewhere in the icy immensity of space.

Addressing the Heart

Here's a practice that's fallen out of fashion:
the poet ardently invoking the heart.

O heart, he calls. Dear heart, she cries,
both caught in the clutches of love.

Never mind that the heart
is about to be scolded
for its long history of foolishness.

Silly heart! the poet chides.
Beware! another warns.
There you go again,
the poet throwing up her hands.

And be still, a wise voice warns
before a kiss at the door
after walking her home in the snow.

Poor, poor heart!
no one talks to you anymore,

much less to the lesser organs.
O kidneys! My foolish lungs!

We no longer even speak to the moon
or the sky, the woods, or the hills
we're so used to murmuring
in the rooms off the hallways within.

O Derwent! cried Wordsworth, to a childhood river,
and his mighty poem was underway in its flow.

BC/AD

One autumn afternoon in the mid-seventies,
when the two realms of Christian time
were still being referred to as BC and AD,
a student of mine raised her hand.

She had found an error in our textbook.
"The dates of Plato are messed up," she said.
"How could he be born in 428 then die in 327?
What, was he going backwards?"

"I suppose you could say that everyone
born before Christ was, in a sense,
going backward in time without knowing it," I said.

Then from the back of the room was heard,
"So did they all start going forward at Christmas?!"
There are moments in a teacher's life
when a discussion has gotten interestingly
out of control and it's time for the allegorical
figure of Reason to enter the stadium
on her docile horse, festooned with facts and numbers.

So while some students joked about the ancients
in their tunics getting younger by the year,

I drew a long horizontal line on the board
to represent all of human time,
then a vertical line intersecting it at the birth of Christ,
and I added a stick figure of Plato standing
on the line and a small zero off to the side.

"You see," I announced, "Plato was born
428 years before the birth of Christ."

"But how did they know that?" she asked.

"Excellent question," I replied, shaking my head.

Then from the back, another excellent one:
"And why do the languages change from English to Latin,
from 'before Christ' to 'Anno Domini.'
You would think it would be the other way around."

"You would think," I repeated,
moving over to the big school window,
one finger pressed pensively to my lips,

to observe the orange and yellow trees,
patches of blue beyond them,
and a few ordinary birds darting through the scene,

until the bell, signaling the end of our class
and the beginning of something else, rang.

This was, after all, an introduction to poetry.

Anniversary

The moment I turned a corner
into a quiet side street
in an unfamiliar city

I ran into the realization
that you had died
exactly nine years ago today,

which led me to envision
a baby who was born
on the same day you died

a boy who would
grow up but always
be the same age as your death

and whose birthday parties
under a tree on a lawn
would be secret memorials to you,

our own imaginary boy
like a breathing statue
in a hidden corner of a park.

This I decided as I leaned
my bicycle against a tree
somewhere in Philadelphia.

Turning the Pages of *A History of Art* the Morning After an Argument

No one is hopping in a painting by Hopper,
not a single rabbit is at play
in a room where a woman in a slip
sits on a bed and stares at the hotel floor.

And no one is at ease in a painting by Bosch
unless howling in a cauldron of boiling oil
with a spear through your head
is someone's idea of contentment.

But here in Constable's airy landscape
Boat-Building near Flatford Mill
a calm sense of peace and purpose prevails.
By a stand of summer trees,

the tiny boat-builder is bent to his labor
in a wide trench dug for the work.
The boat's wooden frame rests
on a cradle of rough-hewn beams.

A smooth English river flows blue
in the background. How smart he was
to be building his boat nearby,
in the light of a calm, cloud-filled sky.

All of which has left me
on this stormy day to imaging my life
as a simple man building his own boat,
not necessarily near Flatford Mill,

but somewhere fairly far away
from the silent rooms of this house.
There, I would speak with the quiet
authority of a nineteenth-century boat-builder.

Villagers would know me by my apron
and the special hat of my trade,
and once in a while, some boys
from the village would come out

to watch me building my boat
then out of youthful boredom
would point and mock my efforts
and hit me in the head with an apple core,

which makes me wonder if you
are ever getting out of bed this morning
so we can have some eggs and toast
and figure out what to do with our Sunday.

Sunday Drive

What if it turns out
that there is no afterlife?
That may come as a letdown to some,
but the good news is
that the believers of every religion
won't experience the least disappointment
for the simple reason
that they will be dead at that point
and incapable of experiencing anything.

Same goes for the skeptics,
agnostics, and the card-carrying atheists.
No opportunity to smirk or brag
for the same reason mentioned above.
I was thinking about this
on my drive to the beach one Sunday
when I saw a flock of well-dressed people
filing into a clapboard church
under a tall, white steeple.

I did not turn the car around,
pull up to the church door,
and deliver this news from the roof of the car.
No, I drove on with the radio up loud
and the windows down,
content to keep those tidings to myself,
a faithless congregation of one,
now driving much too fast
and just as afraid of heaven as he is of hell.

The Guardian

Giovanni Pascoli wrote about this in Italian
before Heaney had a chance
to translate it into English,
so my pencil could wonder about it, too,
a noticing, that is, of the farm dogs
who race barking after every passing cart
or coach, nipping at hooves in a billow of dust.

I've seen such dogs run after a bicycle
or a car, then stop outpaced,
stand still for a moment to make sure
the intruder has gotten the message,
given up any thought of making trouble,
before running back to its post
under a bush or in the shadow of a barn.

Is it madness, this inability to distinguish
between friend or foe, or is it wise,
if you can't tell one from the other,
to run barking madly after everyone
simply to be on the safe side?

Whatever the case, it's a kind of job
and you're free to do it all year round.

And in return, this guardian of family
and farm, roosters and hens,
is rewarded with kibble and scraps
and a porch to sleep under when it rains.
And best of all, he is given a name
that is his and his alone,
enough to turn his head and bring him home.

Lesson Plan

Overcast morning,
cool and grey.
The cat bends low to drink
from the swimming pool
like a tiger at an oasis.
I bend to snip off
a few dead twigs
from a miniature orange tree
with its miniature oranges.
In an hour I will talk
to some students about a poem
I wrote over 30 years ago.
I think I will start off
by telling them about
the miniature orange tree
with its miniature oranges
in a terracotta pot by the pool
and just go from there.

Two

Emily Dickinson in Space

When we were very young,
we heard an Emily Dickinson poem
being recited by our teacher,
then we looked around the classroom at each other.

Later, I graduated to reading one
of her poems every morning
before I rose from my bed with the dawn.

Once in a famous library,
I was allowed to hold a letter she'd written,
and when no one was looking,
I shook it a little, the way
it might have trembled in her hand,
then it began to tremble in mine.

Another time—
and this is harder to believe—
before giving a talk about her
at a university in Rome,
I was introduced by an Italian astronaut

who spoke not from the podium
but from the orbiting space station
saying nice things about me,
as he floated on a big screen,
on holiday from gravity.

Behind him, an oval window
was radiant with the sun's spotless light.

Then he read one of Emily's poems
from a slip of paper in his hand.
There is a solitude of space,
a solitude of sea . . .
a solitude of death . . . Finite infinity.

And when he waved goodbye,
I waved back like a schoolboy
from the front row of the auditorium
in Trastevere, near the flowing Tiber,
then I stood up and gave my earthling talk.

Afterward, a woman told me
the astronaut was none other
than Paolo Nespoli,
who had spent an entire year in space

and who was said to have been
the final lover of the late Oriana Fallaci.

Imagine that, I said to myself,
looking up at the evening sky,
her little poem still circling the globe
at seventeen thousand miles an hour,

hands-down the fastest poem in history
if such records were kept,
passing over everything below
once every ninety-three minutes
including the Vatican and the Colosseum,

not to mention the leafy canopy
of Amherst, Massachusetts, and her small grave
and headstone in the West Cemetery
behind an iron fence, just down an unpaved road.

Eden

I am not Adam
but I was naked in a garden
earlier this morning, which was not
the first morning of human existence,
though it seemed fresh enough
with dewy fronds and a choir of opening flowers,
and there I was, nothing but skin,
walking around the edge of the pool
carrying a green watering can by the handle.

I'm not William Blake either,
he who liked to sit naked with his Catherine
on the enclosed lawn next to their house
waiting for another tree to sprout golden wafers.
Now, there's a man who behaved
as if he actually *were* the first man—
every English dawn unprecedented,
every copper plate a new horizon.

But I did stand there today,
encircled by vegetation,

peering over the low wall of this poem
at the two naked Blakes in their chairs,
who looked back at me with surprise,
a union that lasted for only a tick
before I exited through a gate, returning
to a world of trousers, wooly sweaters, and silly hats.

Being Sonny Rollins

One of the dangers of piping Sonny Rollins
into my earbuds on my morning outing
is that I start wishing that I were Sonny Rollins
as I face again the blunt fact that I am not.

I usually run along a curvy cinder path
on the edge of a lake that sparkles in the sun.
I spot a heron, a pair of ducks, and five white ibises,
but the fact remains that I am still not Sonny Rollins.

I watch hundreds of scattered black birds
wheeling and squawking in the sky
but that cowbell intro to "I'm an Old Cowhand"
reminds me that I am someone other than Sonny Rollins.

Most of the runners and dog walkers
give me some kind of morning greeting.
Then a guy about my age shoots me a look
that says *There's no way you are Sonny Rollins.*

That does it. If I am not Sonny Rollins,
then none of you other people are either.
Not you in the tracksuit or you with the schnauzer—
not one Sonny Rollins in the pack of you.

And so I began exercising the muscles
of sarcasm as I continued to put down
everyone in sight for being inferior
to Sonny Rollins and every other jazz giant,

a pointless habit that ended only
when I found you at home in the kitchen,
you who have no desire to be Sonny Rollins,
you who dream only of being Anita O'Day.

Display Case

By that time,
the body will be ashes,
the warm flesh having gone cold
then set ablaze
and buried in a box,
maybe under a live oak
or delivered to the hands of the wind—
such an unbendable process
may cause a shiver in the night.

But if you've made a mark,
your existence might continue
alphabetically
on a public shelf
or on display in a vitrine,
one visitor after another
peering down at your spectacles
or reading a letter with a misspelling
you once wrote to a gym teacher.

No wonder the little girl
whose father is lifting her up
looks disappointed
by a first edition next to your cane.
But what did she expect
inside the glassed-in case,
something living?
a pair of goldfish
circling in a shiny bowl?

Better hurry by, yourself,
maybe shuffle off to the hall of armor.
Seeing your own worn slippers
might just bring you to tears
if it's possible for the dead
to cry, much less spend
an autumn afternoon
in a museum, invisible,
not even parting the air as they pass.

Fire in the Movies

Is there anyone out there
who can name a movie about a writer
of the eighteenth or nineteenth century
that does not feature a fireplace
into whose manic flames are tossed,
usually one at a time,
the pages of a now lost literary masterpiece?

The scene could be a manor house or a hovel,
fire doesn't know the difference
any more than it can distinguish a voucher
from a poem that could alter the course of literature.

The culprit is usually a rival,
or the wife, driven mad by neglect,
or a mistress, her damp hair in tendrils,
but the best is the author himself
standing transfixed by the mantel
as he consigns his best work to the blaze.

At least that was the case in the movie I saw tonight
where Coleridge is seen burning
the freshly written pages of "Kubla Khan,"
his drug-sunken face flickering above the fire.

I watched it in our house on a brick street
where the only fire is the pilot light
burning in the kitchen stove.

Where my wife just kissed me good night
and where I'm now sitting up in a chair

like a big squirrel with glasses on his nose
concocting a story about how
I killed my only rival in a duel
on a snowy field one Russian winter
one hundred and thirty-five years ago today.

Zero Grannies

By the time I was born
both my grandmothers had died,
so I never got to observe
one of them ironing in a hallway
or sitting on the porch
talking to herself about something or other.

I have no poem to write
about their aprons or their hands.
Oh, those hands, caked with flour,
that baked so many pies
it would take a window sill
a mile long for all of them to cool!

I can't even picture one carrying
her missal to church in the snow
nodding to the sacristan,
while the other one remains confined
to her room for some unknown reason.
Nor can I hear the clicking of their needles.

So reader, you can thank the mortality rate
of nineteenth-century North America
for leaving this poet free to record things
like five birds on a wire,
a lost dog pausing under a street light,
or three lemons doing nothing in a bowl.

Deep Time

You surprised me
when you wheeled a suitcase
out the front door,
calling me a name over your shoulder
before driving off in a cloud of discontent.

Since that occurred,
at least an hour has passed,
and just to give your decision
some historical perspective,
it has been fourteen years since our wedding
and 4 billion years after the appearance of matter.

Yes, you chose to abandon me,
2 billion years after the birth of multicellular life
not to mention 245 million years
since the last dinosaur shook the earth,
and many decades since the invention
of bubble gum, movies, and the fountain pen.

But now I am back in the present,
comforted by the depth of prehistorical time,
leaning against the kitchen sink
and also spinning through infinite space
at an angle of 23.5 degrees

as I examine the details of a rural scene
on the side of this Delft teacup
while waiting for the water to boil
and for you to come back home.

Unless, of course, you are waiting out there
for me to apologize, in which case
you will find yourself all alone at the end
of human time, beholding the tall,
cascading waves of fire, sinkholes of ice,

and that merciless quartet of horsemen
in their scarlet vestments,
who are now wheeling their steeds around
and appear to be galloping furiously in your direction.

The Monet Conundrum

Is every one of these poems
different from the others
he asked himself,
as the rain quieted down,

or are they all the same poem,
haystack after haystack
at different times of day,
different shadows and shades of hay?

Still Life with Fire Engines

Between fires,
they're as still as a speckled pear
or a silver drinking cup
arranged on a damask tablecloth,

though their sheer readiness,
as they peer out of the station,
gives them a certain twitchy aura,
as if each truck somehow extended

into the space about an eighth
of an inch in front of itself,
where it soon *will* be for a second,
then out beyond all things still and composed.

The Cardinal

They say a child might grow up to be an artist
if his sandcastle means nothing
until he leads his mother over for a look.

I'm that way with my wife.
Little things don't mean much
until I report back from the front.

I ran into Rick from the gift shop.
The post office flag is at half-mast.
I counted the cars on a freight train.

Who else in the world would put up
with such froth before it dissolves in the surf?

But early this morning
while I was alone in the pool,
a Vatican-red cardinal flashed down
from the big magnolia
and landed on the deck
right next to where I was standing in the water.

Here was an event worth mentioning,
but better, I considered, to keep this one to myself,
to make it a secret I alone would harbor and possess.

Then I went back to watching the bird
pecking now at the edge of the garden
with the usual swivel-headed wariness of a bird.

I was an unobserved observer
of this private moment,
with only my head above the water,
at very close range for man and bird,
considering my large head and lack of feathers.

A sudden rustling in that tall tree
revealed the grey-and-pink female,
the vigilant mate with whom he shared his life,

but I wouldn't share that with my wife,
not while she buttered toast
or worked the Sunday crossword.
Indeed, I would take the two cardinals to my grave.

In a little while, she appeared on the porch
wearing a bright yellow robe
and carrying two steaming cups of coffee.

We talked about a few ordinary things
as couples do to pass the time.
She told me about her plan to paint her office
and about a party we missed,
and I told her how good the coffee was
and about the two cardinals,
the male pecking in the garden
the female flapping her wings above—
making sure not to leave anything out—
including my idea about keeping it a secret
and that really dumb thing about the grave.

Three

Water, Water

I do some of my best thinking
when standing on the bottom of a lake,
up to my chin in lake water.
I like squinting down the length of it
or staring up at the violet sky.
I don't care if my head looks
like a beachball from the shore,
as long as the lake water holds me up
and I keep my balance with extended arms.
One morning, standing in Lake Ontario,
I could remember no greater happiness.
Unable to contain this feeling, I took
a step and for a moment I was beside myself.

This kind of thing can go on for some time,
thoughts running around my head
like a stampede of antelopes
only sometimes, one of the young stumbles,
and is set upon by a pack of cheetahs.
This is the doomsayer thought
about the future, the lake drying up

and leaving me abandoned, or rising
above its banks to inundate me.
Such are the two most basic human fears,
as if both could not occur at once,
as they do when I dream that I am both
alone and being smothered by a dozen women.

Meanwhile, swimmers swim by
on their way to sunbathe on a raft,
a speedboat lifts me a little in its wake—
all part of life when you are half afloat
and half bouncing off the sandy floor with your toes.
And I'm far enough from shore not to hear
the shouts of foreboding and calamity.
I know the end is near. Seawater
will rise and flood the aquifers,
the basement sofa will begin to float.
So hard to picture it from here, though,
what with the sentinel pines along the shoreline
and just enough water to fill the lake exactly to the brim.

First Typewriter

The old Royal Aristocrat
I got for Christmas long ago
came with its own plastic cover,

so every night at bedtime
I would place the typewriter-shaped
cover over the typewriter

and another cover over the parrot.
Only then, could the three
of us get to sleep.

Then came the night
when I placed the typewriter-
shaped cover over the parrot

and was kept awake for hours
by the sound of her typing
what would turn out to be

the opening lines of *Our Town*
instead of the more customary *Hamlet*
by the more traditional roomful of blind monkeys.

Days of Teenage Glory

When I was busy committing the crime of high school,
the songs on the radio
took about two minutes to play,
and smoking a cigarette took about five,
so that things happened fairly quickly
as we passed the time and it passed us
without a sound except for the singing.

Singing by the Orioles, the Dubs, and the Clovers,
plus Lee Andrews and the Hearts,
who could do no wrong, according to me.

One night in the spring,
I even saw the Jesters battling the Paragons
on the stage of the Brooklyn Paramount,
then wandered the borough in a drizzle.

These days, if I'm not at my desk
or asleep in the back room,
I'm sitting in the garage
with a cup of coffee watching the rain

and waiting for that startling chord
that concludes "He's Gone" by the Chantels,
the five notes the rungs in a ladder
pointed into a vacant teenage sky.

They were students together in the Bronx
at St. Anthony of Padua's school,
but they named themselves
after a rival neighborhood school,
St. Frances de Chantal,
having wisely rejected the Paduas,
as I imagine them doing one afternoon.

Where are the Chantels now?
playing in the snows of yesteryear?
bathing in the waters of childhood?

Are they hanging in the domestic air
like a smoke ring over a kitchen table?
Or like one sailing from a girl's mouth
in a car somewhere
only to vanish in a boy's face
reflected pink in the rearview mirror?

Culture, Textuality, and Space

Early yesterday evening,
as I sat on a downtown train
reading a book titled *Narrativity, Myth, and Revolution,*

I noticed a woman sitting across from me
who was reading an even thicker book
titled *Warfare, Gender, and Historiography.*

What a pair, as my father used to say
about most of my mother's married friends,
particularly a neighbor named Babs

who drank bourbon highballs and crossed her legs
on a couch in my parents' living room
while her husband nursed a ginger ale.

What a pair, I muttered to myself as I rose
for the Astor Place stop
and spotted a man in a wool ski cap

who had his head in a doorstop called
Sexual Identity, Upheaval, and Illusion.
We all deserve each other, I muttered,

stepping onto the platform
and eyeing the red lights on the train
as it bore all the people and their books

into the future—a sudden reminder
that I was running late for tonight's lecture,
"Hyper-Time: Death in the Future of the Future,"

the last in a series of talks that had begun
when the city was simmering hot,
I realized, pulling my scarf tight around my throat.

Crying in Class

This is not a weeping board,
nor a garden of suffering
followed by a hill of greater suffering.
There will be no crying in this class.
That is what the playground is for.

No being held by the wrist,
no animals moaning in the wild.
I'm not going to tell you
what happened on the staircase,
or reveal the hiding places of my childhood.

Everything in this hard place
is designed to disappear.
The moon drops faster than usual
behind a lurid billboard.
A man vanishes from his place on a footbridge.

This is where I was last seen
walking to the town post office
in the shape of a white envelope

and you are forsaken on a platform,
holding an umbrella which has ceased to exist.

If/Then

Let's just say there is no expanding universe,
no quarks and star nurseries,
no cosmic rays and dark matter,

and what if this green earth
were the only planet,
and the sky held nothing
but the sun and the moon,
shining and glowing in their turns,

and maybe only 30 or 40 stars
which you could see
from the porch on a clear night.

Wouldn't it be more reasonable then
to accept that the Creator
would have time and the interest
to listen to everyone's rising prayer:

to be forgiven for an injustice,
for a surgery to go well,

for it to start raining or stop raining,

for a lost pet to find its way home,

or for young Timmy (0–11) to somehow get on base?

Writing in English Is Not the Same as Being English

I felt absolutely nothing
The other evening in Key West
While watching the sun drop colorfully into the Gulf,
And I began to wonder if I would be a better poet
If my father had been a glove maker
Like Shakespeare's, or a chandler, a parson, or a vicar.

Or a hatter like the father of William Collins,
Who was a drunk but wrote "Ode to Evening,"
Before ending up in a madhouse named McDonald's.
What did *my* father do? Well, he was
Not a linen merchant like Alexander Pope's.

Maybe I should have married a milkmaid
And had seven children like John Clare,
Speaking of madhouses. Would that not be
A better preparation for depicting Nature
In all her twigs and thistles, petals and feathers?

Think of how things might have turned out
Had I been schooled at Harrow or Charterhouse,
Or better still, been tubercular, so sickly
As to require a raft of private tutors.
Would I not be better groomed for this life?

Can you picture me coughing
Into a book of blood-flecked eclogues?
Would it help if I added some ruffles and velvet?
But then, I would have to give up my tee shirts
And these orange Hawaiian running shoes,

At once so comfortable and cool-looking.
So never mind. I like being an American.
Imagine, ending up in McDonald's Drive-Thru Madhouse.
Or how about singing Old McDonald *had* a madhouse,
Here a moo, there a moo, everywhere a cluck–cluck!

And my father, no vicar, worked in the city
With an insurance company that funneled
Marine and aviation business into Lloyd's
Of London, where he visited often,
Customarily wearing a hat, and in winter, leather gloves.

New Zealand

It was early evening, the sky a deepening blue,
and we had settled in at a harbor-side table
which a waiter often visited with trays of drinks.
The last thing on my mind was astronomy,
but at one point I tilted back my head
and beheld scattered above me the early stars
of a new hemisphere and, directly overhead,
the twinkling points of the Southern Cross.
What a relief after a lifetime of the Big Dipper
with its odd angles, its bent ladle—
more like a rhomboid on a coat hanger to my eye.
But there is no mistaking the four points of a cross.

The waiter set down another tray of glasses,
and I pictured the scales and the crab,
the altar and the archer, the furnace and the ram,
the small and large dog, the large and small bear—
so many, even if there were only two stars in the sky,
we would have configured them long ago
and lain there staring up on ancient moonless nights
(a whiff of woodsmoke in the air)

contemplating the wonderful simplicity
of Tips of the Horns, the Staring Frog,
or maybe we would just call them the Twins—
that one the boy, and off to the side, his enchanting sister.

The Coronation of the Virgin

I'm well aware of the difference between
the Virgin Birth and the Immaculate Conception,
and I know her son ascended (active voice) into heaven
whereas she was merely assumed (passive voice),
so how could I have missed her coronation?

Here, in Bruyn the Elder's triptych version,
everyone is frozen in their places,
as if they were refrigerated in time,
and instead of looking out at us,
mere mortals in a gallery on a rainy afternoon,

Mary's eyes are lowered, tresses
flowing over her shoulders.
A tall Christ is holding the crown overhead,
his bearded Father lending a hand,
and the Paraclete, who I called the *parakeet*

as a child, hovers enshrined in a wafer.
Is Mary being rewarded for having to watch
her son being nailed to a cross on the ground

then raised—oh, the pain of *that*—
only to bleed out on the top of a hill.

Or was there just the need to dress her up?
I mean we can't have the Mother of God
padding through the clouds in her sandals
wearing the same thing she wore at the Annunciation,
which, it must be said, took her wholly by surprise.

So here she is, going royal in a dark blue robe,
maybe sewn by angels, about to be crowned
much like Elizabeth I and that other Mary,
Queen of Scots. The very word *coronation*
makes me expect the Duke of Edinburgh

to show up in a side panel, dressed for the hunt.
But this tableau is only for divinities,
attended by a rank of winged angels,
yet no rosy toddlers float about
in the painted sky, as blue and clear as yesterday's

here on earth, home of the same trees,
hillsides, and mountains featured in this painting
and everything I am surveying out this window—
the waving palms, trumpeting hibiscus,
and the pale blue rectangle of a swimming pool.

It's a sight not seen anywhere in the New Testament
or in any artistic rendering of heaven,
though I can easily picture those two butterflies
wheeling about in the perfumed air of paradise,
each one wearing his or her miniature golden crown.

The Thing

No ideas but in things.
—WILLIAM CARLOS WILLIAMS

No ideas there either.
—JOHN ASHBERY

It's a Chinese porcelain bowl
alone on a small table
near the big French doors
at the end of a long narrow room.

The bowl reminds me of my mother
because it belonged to her
back when she was alive.

And, later in my life,
before I die,
something else will remind me
of the Chinese bowl and so on.

The room has an echo
because it's empty except for the bowl,
a blue yoga mat,
a fairly huge black piano,

plus a lamp whose base is a monkey
wearing a turban
and looking askance at the whole scene.

But the Chinese bowl
is the thing here and now,
with its hand-painted pictures
of flowers and small birds—

a rooster with a pointy comb,
another with a very long tail
(I had to bend down to look)
all in green, red, white, and even pink.

Breakfast

As I consider the carton of milk
with the picture of Elsie the Cow
suspended over my bowl of cereal,

I'm struck by her friendly grin,
an expression she retains
even in the darkness
of the closed refrigerator.

My cornflakes and berries
are now afloat in the milk
from Elsie's generous udders,

and while I put my spoon to work,
I wonder who wove
the garland of daisies
that encircles her magnificent neck.

Someone on the farm no doubt,
who must have entered the pasture
through a wooden gate

and settled the flowers
over her knobby horns
while Elsie bowed her shapely head.

It seems likely to be
the handiwork of a girl,
maybe one of the daughters,
perhaps an only child.

But where is she now?
In what little town by a river
or on a high mountain
or by a sea shore does she dwell?

What lowing heifer does she now adorn?

The Flâneur

The boulevards are places to ponder,
so he saunters out in the evening
the better to appreciate the crisis of modern life.

I thought I would try this for a while,
but instead of being in Paris, I was in Florida,
so his inspiring sights were not available to me
despite my pledge to aimlessness—

no kiosks or glass-ceilinged arcades,
no beggar with a kerchief covering her hair,
no woman holding her hat down as she crossed a street,
no Victor Hugo look-alike scowling in a greatcoat,

no girls selling fruit or sweets from a cart,
no prostitutes circled under a streetlamp,
no solitude of the moving crowd,
which would drive me to a new kind of sadness.

I did notice a man looking at his watch
and I reflected for a moment on the passage of time,

then I saw two ladies in lime-green and pink
and I considered the fate of the sister arts,
as they stepped into the street arm in arm.

Who needs Europe? I muttered into my foulard
as a boy flew by on a skateboard,
flinging me into a reverie on the folly of youth
and the continuing estrangement of my life.

Poem Interrupted by Gabby Hayes

These offbeat memories,
almost as forgotten as scenery
viewed from a speeding train,
("Yer darn tootin'!")
a blur of leaves, teachers,
mechanics, books I've read,
lamps, racing forms, sheet music,
our secret waterfall.
("What in tarnation?")

But I never worry about the past.
("Did yah hear that, fellers?")
Eventually, the train will slow down
and I will disembark,
light up an autobiographical cigarette
("Now yer talkin'!")
then step into the afterlife,
and disappear into a quizzical haze.
("Well I'll be a possum's grandpa!")

The Horses of Instruction

The tigers of wrath are wiser than the horses of instruction.
—WILLIAM BLAKE

Blake was never more on the money.
Even the ones who managed
to find their classroom
had trouble getting through the door.

They couldn't pick up
a piece of paper or chalk,
and they could count only to 1
or 2 with the thud of a hoof.

But all the students loved to pat
their powerful necks
and ruffle their manes,
and they showed up at every class with an apple.

Thought a Rarity on Paper

Here I am thanking you for this fine copy
of Jack Spicer's posthumous
One Night Stand and Other Poems,
(Grey Fox Press, 1980)
introductions by Donald Allen and Robert Duncan.

It's such a rare little bird,
I was careful to purify my hands
before sliding it out of its clear Mylar sleeve.

I was careful, too, when I turned the pages,
but when Jesus began making out his will
and Alice in Wonderland went missing from the chessboard,
the book had to be restrained from taking flight
and flapping its many wings against a windowpane.

So now, the front cover is bent back a little
like a clam with its shell slightly ajar
the way Spicer's mouth could look sometimes
when we would see him at Gino and Carlo

or in the park by the Church of Sts. Peter and Paul,
where he would often sit cross-legged under a shade tree.

There on hot summer afternoons
he would suffer the company of young poets
if they observed the courtesy of arriving
with cold quart bottles of Rainier ale,
as green as the sports section of the paper.

It was a practice that my friend Tom
and I and his friend A. B. Cole followed religiously.
Spicer even called us "the Jesuits"
for he knew where we had gone to school.

To be imperfectly truthful,
I was intimidated by his reality,
a lonely homosexual adult,
who dressed funnily in summery shirts,
and baggy pants, belt buckle to the side,
his sad moon-face pocked as the moon itself,
and carrying a name like a medieval vendor's.

He would talk about poetics,
of which we knew nothing,
and about the other Berkeley poets,
but we poetry juniors felt more at home

when he talked about Willie McCovey
and we would be on to another still-cold quart.

Then a forceful wind came off the Bay
and blew Jack Spicer away, found a year later at 40
on the floor of an elevator going neither up nor down.

Later still, Tom would be blown over a golden bridge,
his soft inner arm full of holes,
and I sadly lost track of the sardonic Andy Cole.

And here I still remain,
more than twice Spicer's final age,
rolling through the pages of his little book,

listening to his bewildering birds,
and watching Beauty walk, not like a lake,
but among the coffee cups and soup tureens,

causing me to open both my hands
and let this green aeronaut of paper
lift off and fly around my yellow house
and beat its wings against glass
as the thrilling sky continues to change
slowly from blue to black
then, miraculously, back to blue once more.

Four

Beginning

It began in first grade,
all of us staring up
at the *alphabet,* named
after its first two letters, Aa and Bb,

unlike *arithmetic,* not named
after its first two numbers
(putting zero aside)
or *music,* not known as AA sharp,

which is also why
we humans are not known
as AdamEves or EveAdams,
depending on the genetic coin toss—

heads, you're the one waiting
for tails, the waiter,
or vice versa or even versa vice
depending on

the altitude of the coin
and direction of the wind
on that fateful day
back when calculus was only a baby.

Incipit

Too bad this poem wasn't written
in a 12th-century monastic scriptorium
because it would have begun
with a much bigger T,
which would loom over the smaller letters,
their tiny serifs fluttering in the breeze.

The big letter might even be inside
an illuminated scene
perhaps showing in gold two monkeys
or six younger ones hanging
from the crossbar of the T
with vines and flowers growing all around.

More likely, you'd be treated to
the reminder of a skull,
a sheep and shepherd combo,
or the Cross itself, empty now,
with a long winding shroud
draped over its outstretched arms.

But I'd hate to spend my days
hidden under a brown cowl,
writing with a bony, arthritic hand
at a long table of other hooded figures,
then washing down a crust of bread
with medieval water from a dented goblet.

I'd miss my silver car and my stereo
and my wife, who cooks us Cajun shrimp,
so never mind—the plain letter T will do.
Plus, I love being stuck here
in the science fiction of my 21st-century life
even with all the dying around me,

the planet now barely able to spin,
and my pen slithering off into oblivion.

The Peacock

I don't know why the peacock
crossed this ordinary
suburban road, but it took
much longer than any sprinting chicken
would have, due to its substantial tail
and royal, processional gait.

Thus, the people in the head cars
were able to follow its every step
until the long concluding plumage,
with no reason to display its iridescent
fan of eyes, was dragged over the far curb,
following, as always, the resolute body of the bird

wherever it happened to be heading—
to India or ancient Java, I guessed, before stepping on the gas.

Once in a Dog's Age

Just because a dog or a cat or even a hen
doesn't know how old it is
doesn't mean it's not that old.

Every creature moves along
the treadmill of time at its own pace,
most insects hurrying along,
while the tortoise lumbers under its armor.

Many do not look their age
but sometimes you can tell—
take that ancient sparrow
barely moving along as if on crutches.

But what about this crow
on a fence post by the roadside?

No telling how old he is.
Today could be his birthday
for all we know, and who's to say

that perching on a fence post
is not a fine way to celebrate a special day?

My next one's still months away
but when it finally rolls up to the door,
I will remember that crow
of a certain age and join him
on another fence post down the road,

showing off my blue-black feathers,
my shiny head always swiveling
over a field of flowering potatoes
and under an immense silvery sky,

as one car comes and goes,
then another from the other direction.

The Brooklyn Dodgers

Whenever my father
would take me to the ballpark,
I would open up the newspaper
the next morning
to check out the box score,

not to see the hits, runs, and errors,
which I already knew,
but to find the total attendance
and make sure my presence
had been recorded.

The way I saw it,
whatever the total,
I would be the number at the end.

So, if the figure was 24,376,
I would be the 6,
the only one to be
truly counted as an individual.

Without me in the stands,
the number would be a 5,
or if some guy came late,
it would jump to a 7.

I was the one who made it a 6.

And there was my digit
right there on the kitchen table
in black and white,

just the way the typesetter set it,
proof that I existed
and one of my earliest appearances in print.

Frost at the Stove

Like a piece of ice on a hot stove
the poem must ride on its own melting.
—ROBERT FROST

I thought about the simple beauty of this
while I was watching a dollop of butter
glide across the surface of a heated pan,

a more customary sight at the stove,
then tossed in some chopped onions
and when they became translucent,

a bowlful of shrimp, peeled and chilled.
And after the cooking was done,
I pictured Frost sitting down

to his dinner of a heated ice cube—
more like a thimbleful of warm water by now—
while I tied a napkin around my neck

in the manner of a famished coyote,
knife and fork upright in my hands,
then dug into a plate of Louisiana shrimp

resting on a bed of parsley-sprinkled rice,
and raised to the master craftsman
a frosty glass of Chenin Blanc,

carried all the way from France
to accompany another game
happily and carelessly played without a net.

Doctor Jesus

"What if . . ." you said,
handing the joint back to me.
"What if Jesus . . ." you continued,
watching me inhale deeply.
"What if Jesus, instead of being the son of God . . ."
you went on, taking back the joint,
". . . decided he'd rather be a doctor
so his mother would be proud of him."

Neglecting somehow the obvious—
that is, his fabled healing powers—
all I could think to say,
as I looked at you taking a mighty pull,
was "Jesus would look cool
in one of those white doctor's smocks,"
which led to a long silence,
"smock" definitely being the wrong word.

Nonsense

June weekday, abundant sunshine,
vitamin D showering the neighborhood children,

and because I had nothing to write on,
I scratched a poem on the back of a letter
she happened to have written
to say that her many feelings
no longer included any feeling toward me.

My poem was not a response to her,
nor was it in any way about her.
I just happened to write it on the flip side
of her stationery with its silly border of flowers.

What the poem was about were the dry husks
that were dropping into the swimming pool
from the giant magnolia behind the house.

The big white blossoms, some the size of plates,
had had their day, and now
the brown husks were letting go

and falling, one by one,
into that blue-green rectangle of water.

And there they floated, pushed
around by a light breeze
and by the circular force of the pool jets,

and I, luckily, had nothing better to do
than to notice how one husk resembled
a shallop under sail passing an island
where a fair medieval lady was embowered,

while another one appeared cartoonish
and large enough to fit an owl
and a pussycat, leaving plenty of room
for me and an oversized pea-green guitar.

Against Longing

One of the things I would not write is
I wish I could fly away on silver wings
or *I'd like to be a starfish on a sandy beach.*

Longing was once a big part of poetry,
but now it's better to just say you're flying.
I'm flying! And don't sound overly surprised by it.

Then you can describe all the things
you find yourself flying over.
Another baseball diamond . . . and that marina.

And as for the nagging ambition
to be a starfish lying on a sandy beach,
just *be* one, lying there on a summer day

in the middle of a circle of little kids,
all poking you with sticks
until some older kid comes along,

picks you up, and launches you underhand
in a huge arc back into the sea.
Poof, you're a starfish.

Also, you don't need that extra word *sandy*.
Let the reader make the beach sandy
in his head, let him meet you part way.

You can even picture your reader
alone in a poorly lit public library
looking down at your poems the way

those kids looked down at you on the beach,
wondering how you were ever born
and how you manage to get from place to place.

Margins

I cannot thank you enough,
so I will thank you insufficiently,
for the book full of reproductions
of the whimsical drawings found
in the margins of medieval manuscripts,
which you gave me the last time we met for ice cream.

I love turning the colorful pages
and seeing the tiny scribal adornments,
especially of animals still around today—
the robin, the frog, the spoonbill, and the hen,
not to mention the goose, the fox, and the partridge,
all surviving in our meadows, swamps, and barnyards.

I also enjoyed the half-boy blowing a horn
and the four monks rowing a rowboat,
but I would really like to meet the guy
who distracted himself one morning
early in the thirteenth century
from the arduous job of copying the *Alphonso Psalter*

by drawing a monkey doing a handstand
on the back of a comely mermaid
as she is offering a breast to a nursing baby.
I'd like to buy that man a few flagons
and a slice of venison to chew on
as we got to know one another in his favorite pub.

He would introduce me to his friends,
a ploughman, a merchant, and a wayward prioress,
and I would refrain from telling him
about motion pictures and moon landings.
After a while, light would leave the windows
and the ruddy publican would call the time.

Then outside under the sign, as we said goodbye
I would add "But in the end, of course,
life is not all hand-standing monkeys
and comely nursing mermaids."
"It isn't?!" he would shoot back with a booming laugh,
which would leave me nonplussed as I walked back

past printing presses, guillotines, microscopes,
locomotives, radios, and ice cream parlors,
all the way up to the encircling arms of the present.

Drawing a Pineapple

The assignment was to draw a pineapple,
but I began with some scruffy hedges
and a cluster of maples in the background,

for I had made the mistake of picturing
the pineapple outdoors instead of
on the table where it clearly had been placed.

And that led me to include
a chain of low mountains in the distance
and some lighter ones beyond them,

and what still life would be complete
without a sun emitting shine-lines in the sky?
I asked, but no one answered.

And so I persisted, adding some clouds,
shaded on their undersides,
and even a few airborne seagulls,

all part of the ever-expanding sphere
of my sketch pad, until my runaway pencil
vanished into a little point in the distance.

Poor pineapple, I realize now,
overlooked symbol of hospitality,
sculpted fruit of welcome by the door,

reduced now to a dot in a landscape,
forgive my adolescent pencil
in its eagerness to explore the world

for bypassing the simple fact of you,
for not seeing the world that you are—
the rough armadillo plates of your surface

and your pale yellow, succulent interior
waiting on a rudimentary table
for the unstoppable downswing of the blade.

Autobiography

This morning, I began writing mine,
but five hours and many legal pads later
I had gotten only as far as my conveyance
from the French Hospital to my parents' apartment.

Of course, I could have devoted less time
to the bodily process of my birth,
the details of my wicker bassinet

as well as the many metallic animals
endlessly circling above me
as I lay supine, helpless and staring.

And so after a sandwich for lunch,
with so much work ahead of me,
including a catalogue raisonné of my toys
and a count of the tiles on the bathroom wall
behind which once resided my imaginary friend,

I decided to abandon the whole project
and maybe settle for a little essay
on the subject of the wallpaper or the taste of prunes.

Plus I already could hear
the voices of the vicious reviewers
happy to dwell on my shortcomings—

my love of personification
(my melancholic tricycle, for instance),
the limits of the first-person-selfish
point of view, not to mention
the overall lack of a clear theme.

And they would be right
about the pages and pages of senseless dialogue,
not to mention the tedium of chronological order,
even though that seems to be the way
my life has chosen to unfold itself, at least so far.

Your Poem

The choice of season is up to you,
though winter is best for poetry,
and you can pick any time of day—
not just my favorites, dawn or late afternoon,
and mention the day of the week, if you like.

What emotion I was feeling at the time
I would leave up to you as well,
buoyant ease in the shadow of mortality
being one of many options, the mixing
of the sugar of joy and the salt of sorrow another.

Whether I was standing, sitting,
or supine, I also place in your hands.

Where we are located is another matter.
You're in charge now. Entirely your call.
The choices here can be overwhelming
in a world of at least 10,000 places,
so don't hurry your selection with this one.

Train windows and rooftops are good.
Or you could pick a beach scene,
a solitary swimmer, arm bent above a wave.
Toss in some shells, whatever you think works.
The pen is in your hand.
You're up there in the driver's seat.

I'm not even here anymore.
I'm somewhere else,
leaning against a tree, as it happens.
It's a Monday around dusk.
Some yellow leaves float down.
I'm 27. A dog stretching at my side.

After a Morning Shower

When I dry off
by flapping
a big white towel
in front of myself,

I could be a naked man
on a sinking raft
a thousand miles from shore
with only a white towel

to signal a tiny freighter
heading for the horizon—
yes, a naked man who now,
thanks to his vigorous flapping,

finds himself a little more
than a thousand miles from shore.

Daydream

Now we are nearing the end of the final exam
here in early June, named after Juno,
the Roman goddess of examinations,
a time when the trees seem surprised
at how green they have become
and all kinds of flora are springing up in the yards.

Azaleas, for example, are very common,
and you remember the colors
of the ones you saw this morning
in the neighbor's yard on your walk to school—
red, white, and bright pink—
the neighbor with the tall daughter

whose hand you once held in the dark,
the silence so deep on the porch swing that night,
just the whisper of a breeze,
the sound of her breathing against yours,
then the voice of an adult instructing
the class to look up and put down your pencils.

Reading the Guest Book

For some of the departing guests
it took only a line or two
to express their thanks and add some flattery,
using the handy ballpoint pen on the hall table.

Others needed a whole page
to detail the many agreeable aspects
of the place—the comfy bed, the spice rack,
the traffic of birds around the feeder.
And sometimes a child had left
near the bottom of a page
a drawing of a sailboat or a pine tree
for this was a cottage in the woods by a lake.

The content was pretty much the same
for all agreed the place was exceedingly lovely;
indeed, as I turned the pages,
it seemed the cottage and the woods and lake
had been growing more and more lovely
with every passing summer

as if everyone, like me, read the whole book
and now was resolved to outdo the previous entries,
piling up one superlative after another
to create a state of such perfection
that the comments might have been left
by Adam or Eve before they fled paradise
through what was then the world's only gate.

For surely, our first parents
enjoyed their all-too-brief stay
as much as the Larsen family had enjoyed theirs.
Like the Ryans on their honeymoon,
they must have appreciated the scenery.
And like the Talbots, the Halvorsons from Wisconsin,
and the Blancos from Philadelphia,
they too couldn't wait to come back another time.

Of course, there would be no coming back
because of the talking snake coiled around a fruit tree
and the flood of human shame that followed.

And leave it to the guest book
to contain another fall from grace
experienced just last summer
by one of the Stokes family from Jackson Heights,

young Emily, who wrote in her best penmanship
"Sorry about your little blue vase.
I was just trying to put some flowers in."

And then, with a bag packed at my side,
it was my turn with the ballpoint pen,
but all I could think about
were the shards of the blue vase
scattered on the tiles of the kitchen floor
as well as the pool of water spilled there
and the various wildflowers still in her hand.

A Change of Heart

I once expressed the wish for a tomb
topped by a white marble angel,
her head buried in her folded wing,
but now, I'd rather you

just copy out that little poem by Ryota,
fold it into quarters,
then slip it into my shirt pocket
before I am incinerated in a chamber.

It's the one where he used to think
that death came only to others,
but now in his ultimate hour,
he realizes that this happiness is also his.

Acknowledgments

My thanks to the editors of the following periodicals, where some of these poems first appeared:

The Atlantic: "Ode to Joy"
Brilliant Corners: "While in Amsterdam"
Ecotone: "New Zealand"
Five Points: "Addressing the Heart," "Aubade," "Beginning," "First Typewriter," "The Guardian," "The Monet Conundrum," "Sunday Drive"
The New Republic: "Lesson Plan," "Marijuana"
The New Yorker: "Days of Teenage Glory," "Incipit," "Thought a Rarity on Paper"
New Ohio Review: "The Cardinal"
Poetry East: "Eden," "Zero Grannies"
The Southampton Review: "Doctor Jesus," "The Horses of Instruction," "Once in a Dog's Age," "Poem Interrupted by Gabby Hayes," "Winter Trivia"

"The Coronation of the Virgin" appeared in *The Map of Every Lilac Leaf: Poets Respond to the Smith College Museum of Art,* ed. Matt Donovan (SCMA, 2018).

"Your Poem" appeared in *Hwaet! 20 Years of Ledbury Poetry Festival*, ed. Mark Fisher (Bloodaxe Books, 2016).

"The Monet Conundrum" was chosen by Mary Jo Salter for *Best American Poetry 2024.*

I am grateful to everyone at Random House who worked to bring this book into being, especially my astute, empathetic editor, David Ebershoff. Thanks to Chris Calhoun for his friendship and unflagging advocacy, and to my devoted wife, Suzannah, for her advice and care on too many levels to mention.

Note: The poet in "A Change of Heart" is Oshima Ryota (1718–1787).

ABOUT THE AUTHOR

BILLY COLLINS is a former Poet Laureate of the United States. He is the author of twelve collections of poetry, including the bestsellers *Aimless Love, The Trouble with Poetry,* and *Sailing Alone Around the Room.* He is also the editor of *Poetry 180, 180 More,* and *Bright Wings.* A former Distinguished Professor at Lehman College of the City University of New York, Collins served as New York State Poet from 2004 to 2006. In 2016 he was inducted into the American Academy of Arts and Letters. He lives in Florida with his wife, Suzannah.